Whale Shark

GIANTS of the **OCEAN**

Sue LeBreton

AV2 BY WEIGL™
MEDIA ENHANCED BOOKS
ADDED VALUE · AUDIO VISUAL

www.av2books.com

AV² provides enriched content that supplements and complements this book. Weigl's AV² books strive to create inspired learning and engage young minds in a total learning experience.

Your AV² Media Enhanced books come alive with...

Audio
Listen to sections of the book read aloud.

Key Words
Study vocabulary, and complete a matching word activity.

Video
Watch informative video clips.

Quizzes
Test your knowledge.

Go to **www.av2books.com**, and enter this book's unique code.

Embedded Weblinks
Gain additional information for research.

Slide Show
View images and captions, and prepare a presentation.

BOOK CODE

V 5 1 1 6 3 0

Try This!
Complete activities and hands-on experiments.

... and much, much more!

AV² by Weigl brings you media enhanced books that support active learning.

Published by AV2 by Weigl.
350 5th Avenue, 59th Floor New York, NY 10118
Websites: www.av2books.com   www.weigl.com

Library of Congress Cataloging-in-Publication Data

LeBreton, Sue.
 Whale shark / Sue LeBreton.
   pages cm. -- (Giants of the ocean)
Includes index.
ISBN 978-1-4896-1082-9 (hardcover : alk. paper) -- ISBN 978-1-4896-1083-6 (softcover : alk. paper) --
ISBN 978-1-4896-1084-3 (ebk.) -- ISBN 978-1-4896-1085-0 (ebk.)
1. Whale shark--Juvenile literature. I. Title.
QL638.95.R4L43 2015
597.3'3--dc23

                        2014004623

Printed in the United States of America in North Mankato, Minnesota
1 2 3 4 5 6 7 8 9 0 18 17 16 15 14

042014
WEP150314

Senior Editor: Heather Kissock
Design: Mandy Christiansen

Weigl acknowledges Getty Images as the primary image supplier for this title.

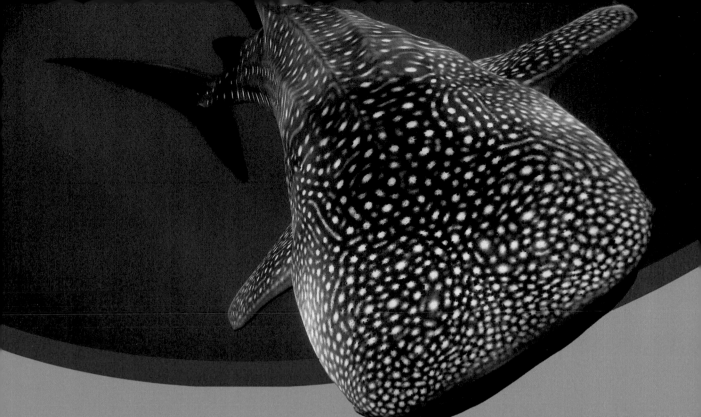

Contents

Meet the Whale Shark

Even though their name suggests otherwise, whale sharks are not whales. They are fish. The word whale describes their size. The whale shark is the largest fish in the ocean. In fact, it may be the largest type of fish that has ever lived.

A whale shark, like other fish, breathes underwater through its gills. It swims near the surface with its mouth open and sucks in water, **plankton**, and other small fish. The gills trap food and let the water pass through. Although the whale shark has thousands of teeth, it does not chew or tear its food. The whale shark swallows the trapped food whole or in chunks.

Whale sharks are dark on the upper side of their bodies and lighter on the underside. This provides **camouflage** from enemies. Each whale shark has a unique checkerboard pattern of light stripes and spots on its upper side. Today, scientists use these patterns to identify and track individual sharks.

Whale sharks have several hard ridges called "keels" on their backs.

All About Whale Sharks

Whale sharks belong to the Orectolobiformes order. Fish in this order are sometimes called carpet sharks. This is because they have markings that look like the patterns in a carpet.

Where Whale Sharks Live

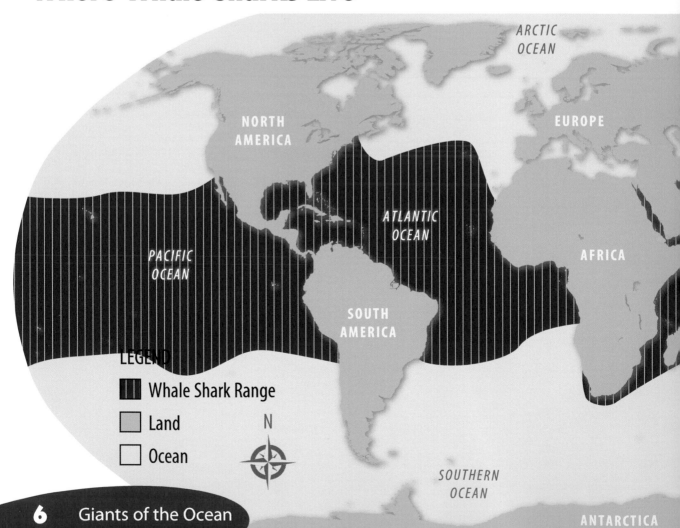

ARCTIC OCEAN

NORTH AMERICA

EUROPE

ATLANTIC OCEAN

PACIFIC OCEAN

AFRICA

SOUTH AMERICA

LEGEND

■ Whale Shark Range

■ Land

□ Ocean

N

SOUTHERN OCEAN

ANTARCTICA

All sharks in this order share certain features. They all have eyes behind their mouths, five pairs of gills, and two, triangle-shaped **dorsal** fins on their backs. These fins prevent the whale shark from rolling as it swims. The fins also help the whale shark stop and turn quickly.

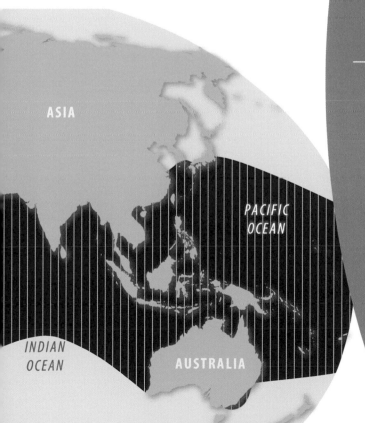

20 to 40 feet (6 to 12 meters) long on average

Mouth alone can be **5 feet** (1.5 m) wide

Can weigh up to **26,000 pounds** (11,800 kilograms)

Can live **60** to **100** years

Classifying Whale Sharks

ORDER
Orectolobiformes

FAMILY
Rhincodontidae

GENUS
Rhincodon

SPECIES
Typus

ASIA

PACIFIC OCEAN

INDIAN OCEAN

AUSTRALIA

The Home of
Whale Sharks

Whale sharks live in the warm waters of **tropical** and **subtropical** seas. They are found both in the open sea and close to shore. Whale sharks are usually seen feeding near the surface, but they can dive into waters more than 3,280 feet (1,000 m) deep.

In the spring, whale sharks **migrate** to areas rich in fish eggs. They swim thousands of miles (kilometers) to arrive in seas where fish or coral are **spawning**. Here, they feed on the eggs.

During spawning season, whale sharks can be seen in areas such as Gladden Spit in Belize, Ningaloo Reef in Western Australia, and Batangas in the Philippines. In 2011, scientists counted 420 whale sharks feasting in the waters off the coast of Mexico. Before the 1980s, fewer than 350 whale sharks had ever been seen in the world.

Scientists believe that whale sharks **live alone**.

While whale sharks are solitary animals, they sometimes come together in schools of more than 100.

Features of Whale Sharks

EYES
A whale shark's eyes do not blink. When something comes too close to the eye, the eyeball falls back into the shark's head, and a tough flap of skin comes forward to protect the eye.

Whale sharks have several **adaptations** that allow them to survive in their watery **habitat**. Some features help them feed. Others help them stay warm.

MOUTH
Most sharks have mouths on the underside of their heads. The mouth of a whale shark is different. It is located at the front of the shark's broad, flat head. Using its wide mouth, the whale shark can scoop up large amounts of plankton and small fish as it swims along.

SPIRACLE

The spiracle is a small slit in front of the five large gill slits. This slit allows the whale shark to take in water and draw out oxygen. The whale shark can then continue breathing even when it is resting on the sea floor.

SKIN

The skin of adult whale sharks is up to 4 inches (10 centimeters) thick. It is covered with scales that feel like sandpaper. **Predators** find it difficult to bite into this armor. A layer of fat below the skin keeps the shark warm when it is hunting in cold, deep waters.

SKELETON

A whale shark's skeleton is made of **cartilage**, not bone. Cartilage is more flexible than bone. It allows the whale shark to move easily through the water.

Diet of
Whale
Sharks

Whale sharks are **carnivores**. They eat plankton and tiny fish such as sardines, anchovies, and even small tuna. Whale sharks are also **filter feeders** and are one of only three types of sharks that feed this way.

A whale shark has about **3,000 tiny teeth** in its mouth. The teeth serve no known purpose.

When feeding at the surface, whale sharks bob up and down, sucking food into their mouths. However, whale sharks also dive deep looking for fish eggs. In Belize, scientists have seen whale sharks stay in shallow water eating plankton during the cool night. In the day, they dive into deep and cooler waters to escape the heat.

For decades, fishers knew that whale sharks met regularly at special places to feed. Working together, scientists and fishers learned that whale sharks come yearly to Gladden Spit. They eat the eggs of the cubera snapper and other fish that spawn there. The whale sharks come after a full moon and stay up to 10 days each spring.

Schools of fish sometimes swim next to whale sharks for protection.

Life Cycle of Whale Sharks

Much of the whale shark's life cycle is a mystery. Scientists think whale sharks live 60 to 100 years, maybe even 150 years. Whale sharks grow quickly after birth, but their growth rate slows as they get older. They are considered adult when they are between 25 and 30 years old or about 26 feet (8 m) long.

Scientists do not know how often whale sharks breed, nor do they know the length of the **gestation** period. No mating or birthing ground for whale sharks has ever been found. Mature female whale sharks have rarely been seen nature. More research is needed to better understand the whale shark life cycle.

The Cycle

Whale Sharks Mate
Whale sharks mate when they are 25 to 30 years old.

Female Becomes Pregnant
Female whale sharks can carry as many as 300 eggs.

Giving Birth
The female gives birth to live **pups**. Live pups are on their own to hunt and survive.

The Eggs Hatch
Whale shark eggs develop and hatch inside the female.

History of Whale Sharks

Whale sharks have roamed the seas for millions of years. In 1828, a whale shark was caught in Table Bay, South Africa. The fish was then named and described by Andrew Smith, a military doctor. The shark was small, measuring just 15 feet (4.6 m). That whale shark is preserved and can be seen today at the Natural History Museum in Paris.

The whale shark's scientific name is *rhincodon typus*, meaning "snout-toothed." The whale part of its common name was given because it is as big as a whale and it filter feeds like some whales. The shark name was given because the fish has cartilage, not bone, making it a true shark.

Whale sharks have been seen traveling in the waters off the coasts of more than 100 countries. They are protected in about 13 countries, including the United States, Australia, India, and the Philippines. The more scientists learn about whale sharks and their movements, the more people will be able to protect them.

Whale sharks sometimes come close to divers and snorkelers, who are dwarfed by the immense size of the shark.

Encounters with Whale Sharks

Whale sharks have not been well studied because they are rarely seen. There have been only several hundred sightings of whale sharks throughout the world. Based on these numbers, scientists believe the number of whale sharks is low.

In 2001, a female whale shark was tracked taking a **8000-mile** (7,200-km) trip across the Pacific Ocean.

Today, scientists use high-tech tools to track how and where whale sharks move and feed. These tools have increased the amount of information that scientists are able to collect about these mysterious fish. One tool, a satellite-linked tag, is placed on a whale shark's fin. It records temperature, water pressure, and light levels. After a set time, the tag comes off the shark and floats to the surface. The tag emails the information it has collected to scientists.

This tracking has given scientists more detail about the whale shark. Scientists now know that whale sharks will swim across an ocean in search of food. They also understand how important spawning areas are to the whale sharks. As a result, scientists can make better plans to protect both these spawning habitats and the whale sharks when they are feeding at these sites.

Tagging whale sharks has helped scientists learn more about their migration patterns.

Conservation

The **International Union for Conservation of Nature (IUCN)** lists whale sharks as vulnerable. This means they are in danger of extinction. The main threat they face is from fishers. Whale sharks are often hunted for their fins. In this type of fishing, called finning, the fins are removed, and the rest of the shark is thrown back into the ocean to die. The shark fins are then used to make shark fin soup, a dish popular in Asia, Australia, and Hawai'i.

Many countries have laws to protect the whale shark. In 2011, President Obama signed the Shark Conservation Act into law. The law is meant to stop shark finning in the United States. The United States also has a ban on fishing whale sharks along the eastern seaboard.

Myths and Legends

In Kenyan legend, the whale shark is called "papa shilling," meaning "shark covered in shillings." A shilling is a type of coin. The legend says that when God made the whale shark, he was so happy with it that he gave the angels gold and silver coins to throw from heaven onto its back. This is why the whale shark has its mysterious markings. When the markings catch the sunlight and sparkle, the shark is believed to be saying "Thank you."

In Vietnam, the whale shark is worshiped as a god. Called Ca Ong, the shark is believed to provide protection to fishers while they are on the water. It can also bring them good fishing. Fishers often build **altars** on the beach to pray to Ca Ong.

The Japanese call the whale shark *ebisuzame*. They consider the fish to be a good luck charm. Japanese fishers are careful not to catch the whale shark or bring it to harm. They do not want to bring bad luck upon themselves.

Even though sharks can be seen as dangerous animals, the whale shark is different. Many people view it as a calm, gentle creature. In India, it is sometimes called Vhali, or "dear one." Worldwide, it is often referred to as the "gentle giant" of the sea.

Test Your Knowledge

The whale shark is one of more than 400 species of sharks living in the ocean. The activity below will help you learn more about these different types of sharks. You will need two blank sheets of paper and a pencil or a pen.

Materials

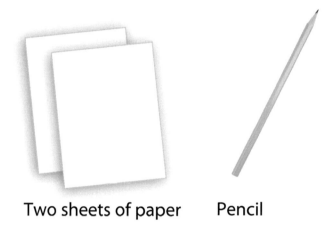

Two sheets of paper   Pencil

1 Using this book and other resources, read about different species of sharks and their characteristics.

2 Now using what you have learned, draw a picture of four different shark species on the first sheet of paper. Label your drawings with the name of each type of shark.

3 On the second sheet of paper, write the names of the species of the sharks you drew across the top of the paper. Then, in point form, write down how these species are similar to and different from each other.

Quiz

1 Are whale sharks whales or fish?

2 How many gills does a whale shark have on each side of its head?

3 Is the pattern on the back of whale sharks the same on all whale sharks?

4 How long was the largest whale shark ever measured?

5 Are whale sharks found in the open sea or close to shore?

6 How big is the whale shark's mouth?

7 Why do whale sharks have teeth?

8 What is a whale shark skeleton made of?

9 What type of feeder is a whale shark?

10 How many countries do whale sharks pass by?

Answers:
1. Fish 2. Five 3. No 4. 44.29 feet (13.5 m) 5. Both 6. About 4 to 6 feet (1.2 to 2 m) across 7. Scientists do not know 8. Cartilage 9. A filter feeder 10. More than 100

Key Words

adaptations: changes that help an animal or plant survive

altars: places to worship or praise

camouflage: to hide an animal, person, or place

carnivores: animals that eat other animals

cartilage: a strong, flexible material that forms some body parts in animals

dorsal: on or near the back part of the body

filter feeders: animals that feed by straining food from water, usually through their gills

gestation: the time of development inside the female until birth

habitat: the natural environment of an organism

International Union for Conservation of Nature (IUCN): the largest and oldest organization in the world dedicated to conserving the environment

migrate: to move from one place to another

plankton: very small plants and animals that float in oceans and lakes

predators: animals that hunt other animals for food

pups: baby whale sharks

spawning: depositing eggs

subtropical: near the tropics

tropical: areas where it is very hot or humid

Index

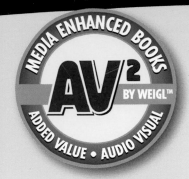

Log on to www.av2books.com

AV² by Weigl brings you media enhanced books that support active learning. Go to www.av2books.com, and enter the special code found on page 2 of this book. You will gain access to enriched and enhanced content that supplements and complements this book. Content includes video, audio, weblinks, quizzes, a slide show, and activities.

AV² Online Navigation

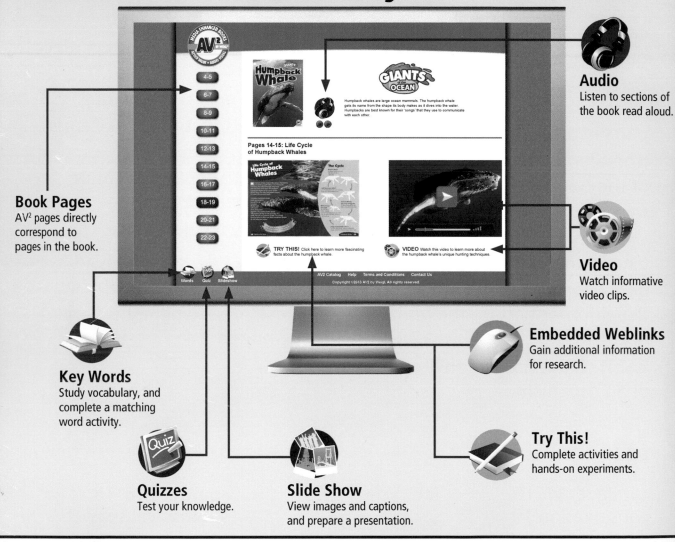

Audio
Listen to sections of the book read aloud.

Book Pages
AV² pages directly correspond to pages in the book.

Video
Watch informative video clips.

Key Words
Study vocabulary, and complete a matching word activity.

Embedded Weblinks
Gain additional information for research.

Quizzes
Test your knowledge.

Slide Show
View images and captions, and prepare a presentation.

Try This!
Complete activities and hands-on experiments.

AV² was built to bridge the gap between print and digital. We encourage you to tell us what you like and what you want to see in the future.

Sign up to be an AV² Ambassador at www.av2books.com/ambassador.

Due to the dynamic nature of the Internet, some of the URLs and activities provided as part of AV² by Weigl may have changed or ceased to exist. AV² by Weigl accepts no responsibility for any such changes. All media enhanced books are regularly monitored to update addresses and sites in a timely manner. Contact AV² by Weigl at 1-866-649-3445 or av2books@weigl.com with any questions, comments, or feedback.